In
1935 if you wanted to
read a good book, you needed
either a lot of money or a library card.
Cheap paperbacks were available, but their
poor production generally mirrored the quality
between the covers. One weekend that year,
Allen Lane, Managing Director of The Bodley Head,
having spent the weekend visiting Agatha Christie,
found himself on a platform at Exeter station trying to
find something to read for his journey back to London.
He was appalled by the quality of the material he had to
choose from. Everything that Allen Lane achieved from that
day until his death in 1970 was based on a passionate belief
in the existence of 'a vast reading public for *intelligent*
books at a low price'. The result of his momentous vision
was the birth not only of Penguin, but of the 'paperback
revolution'. Quality writing became available for the price of
a packet of cigarettes, literature became a mass medium
for the first time, a nation of book-borrowers became a
nation of book-buyers – and the very concept of book
publishing was changed for ever. Those founding
principles – of quality and value, with an overarching
belief in the fundamental importance of reading –
have guided everything the company has
done since 1935. Sir Allen Lane's
pioneering spirit is still very much alive
at Penguin in 2005. Here's to
the next 70 years!

MORE THAN A BUSINESS

'We decided it was time to end the almost customary half-hearted manner in which cheap editions were produced – as though the only people who could possibly want cheap editions must belong to a lower order of intelligence. We, however, believed in the existence in this country of a vast reading public for intelligent books at a low price, and staked everything on it'
Sir Allen Lane, 1902–1970

'The Penguin Books are splendid value for sixpence, so splendid that if other publishers had any sense they would combine against them and suppress them'
George Orwell

'More than a business ... a national cultural asset'
Guardian

'When you look at the whole Penguin achievement you know that it constitutes, in action, one of the more democratic successes of our recent social history'
Richard Hoggart

Idiot Nation

MICHAEL MOORE

PENGUIN BOOKS

PENGUIN BOOKS

Published by the Penguin Group
Penguin Books Ltd, 80 Strand, London WC2R 0RL, England
Penguin Group (USA) Inc., 375 Hudson Street, New York, New York 10014, USA
Penguin Group (Canada), 10 Alcorn Avenue, Toronto, Ontario, Canada M4V 3B2
(a division of Pearson Penguin Canada Inc.)
Penguin Ireland, 25 St Stephen's Green, Dublin 2, Ireland
(a division of Penguin Books Ltd)
Penguin Group (Australia), 250 Camberwell Road, Camberwell, Victoria 3124,
Australia (a division of Pearson Australia Group Pty Ltd)
Penguin Books India Pvt Ltd, 11 Community Centre,
Panchsheel Park, New Delhi – 110 017, India
Penguin Group (NZ), cnr Airborne and Rosedale Roads, Albany,
Auckland 1310, New Zealand (a division of Pearson New Zealand Ltd)
Penguin Books (South Africa) (Pty) Ltd, 24 Sturdee Avenue,
Rosebank 2196, South Africa

Penguin Books Ltd, Registered Offices: 80 Strand, London WC2R 0RL, England

www.penguin.com

Stupid White Men first published in the USA by Regan Books 2001
First published in Penguin Books 2002
This extract published as a Pocket Penguin 2005

1

Set in 11.5/13.5pt Monotype Dante
Typeset by Palimpsest Book Production Limited
Polmont, Stirlingshire
Printed in England by Clays Ltd, St Ives plc

Idiot Nation

Do you feel like you live in a nation of idiots?

I used to console myself about the state of stupidity in this country by repeating this to myself: *Even if there are two hundred million stone-cold idiots in this country, that leaves at least eighty million who'll get what I'm saying – and that's still more than the populations of the United Kingdom and Iceland combined!*

Then came the day I found myself sharing an office with the ESPN game show *Two-Minute Drill*. This is the show that tests your knowledge of not only who plays what position for which team, but who hit what where in a 1925 game between Boston and New York, who was rookie of the year in 1965 in the old American Basketball Association, and what Jake Wood had for breakfast the morning of May 12, 1967.

I don't know the answer to any of those questions – but for some reason I do remember Jake Wood's uniform number: 2. Why on earth am I retaining that useless fact?

I don't know, but after watching scores of guys waiting to audition for that ESPN show, I think

I do know something about intelligence and the American mind. Hordes of these jocks and lunkheads hang out in our hallway awaiting their big moment, going over hundreds of facts and statistics in their heads and challenging each other with questions I can't see why anyone would be able to answer other than God Almighty Himself. To look at these testosterone-loaded bruisers you would guess that they were a bunch of illiterates who would be lucky if they could read the label on a Bud.

In fact, they are geniuses. They can answer all thirty obscure trivia questions in less than 120 seconds. That's four seconds a question – including the time used by the slow-reading celebrity athletes who ask the questions.

I once heard the linguist and political writer Noam Chomsky say that if you want proof the American people aren't stupid, just turn on any sports talk radio show and listen to the incredible retention of facts. It is amazing – and it's proof that the American mind is alive and well. It just isn't challenged with anything interesting or exciting. *Our* challenge, Chomsky said, was to find a way to make politics as gripping and engaging as sports. When we do that, watch how Americans will do nothing but talk about who did what to whom at the WTO.

But first, they have to be able to read the letters *WTO*.

There are forty-four million Americans who cannot read and write above a fourth-grade level – in other words, who are functional illiterates.

How did I learn this statistic? Well, I *read* it. And now you've read it. So we've already eaten into the mere 99 hours a *year* an average American adult spends reading a book – compared with 1,460 hours watching television.

I've also read that only 11 percent of the American public bothers to *read* a daily newspaper, beyond the funny pages or the used car ads.

So if you live in a country where forty-four million can't read – and perhaps close to another two hundred million can read but usually don't – well, friends, you and I are living in one very scary place. A nation that not only churns out illiterate students BUT GOES OUT OF ITS WAY TO REMAIN IGNORANT AND STUPID is a nation that should not be running the world – at least not until a majority of its citizens can locate Kosovo (or any other country it has bombed) on the map.

It comes as no surprise to foreigners that Americans, who love to revel in their stupidity, would 'elect' a president who rarely reads *anything* – including his own briefing papers – and thinks Africa is a nation, not a continent. An idiot leader of an idiot nation. In our glorious land of plenty, less is always more when it comes to taxing any lobe of the brain with the intake of facts and numbers, critical thinking, or the comprehension of anything that isn't . . . well, sports.

Our Idiot-in-Chief does nothing to hide his ignorance – he even brags about it. During his commencement address to the Yale Class of 2001, George W. Bush spoke proudly of having been a mediocre student at Yale. 'And to the C students, I say you, too, can be President of the United States!' The part where you also need an ex-President father, a brother as governor of a state with missing ballots, and a Supreme Court full of your dad's buddies must have been too complicated to bother with in a short speech.

As Americans, we have quite a proud tradition of being represented by ignorant high-ranking officials. In 1956 President Dwight D. Eisenhower's nominee as ambassador to Ceylon (now Sri Lanka) was unable to identify either the country's prime minister or its capital during his Senate confirmation hearing. Not a problem – Maxwell Gluck was confirmed anyway. In 1981 President Ronald Reagan's nominee for deputy secretary of state, William Clark, admitted to a wide-ranging lack of knowledge about foreign affairs at his confirmation hearing. Clark had no idea how our allies in Western

Europe felt about having American nuclear missiles based there, and didn't know the names of the prime ministers of South Africa or Zimbabwe. Not to worry – he was confirmed, too. All this just paved the way for Baby Bush, who hadn't quite absorbed the names of the leaders of India or Pakistan, two of the seven nations that possess the atomic bomb.

And Bush went to Yale *and* Harvard.

Recently a group of 556 seniors at fifty-five prestigious American universities (e.g., Harvard, Yale, Stanford) were given a multiple-choice test consisting of questions that were described as 'high school level.' Thirty-four questions were asked. These top students could only answer 53 percent of them correctly. And only one student got them all right.

A whopping 40 percent of these students did not know when the Civil War took place – even when given a wide range of choices: A. 1750–1800; B. 1800–1850; C. 1850–1900; D. 1900–1950; or E. after 1950. (*The answer is C, guys*.) The two questions the college seniors scored highest on were (1) Who is Snoop Doggy Dog? (98 percent got that one right), and (2) Who are Beavis and Butthead? (99 percent knew). For my money, Beavis and Butthead represented some of the best American satire of the nineties, and Snoop and his fellow rappers have much to say about America's social ills, so I'm not going down the road of blaming MTV.

What I *am* concerned with is why politicians like Senators Joe Lieberman of Connecticut and Herbert Kohl of Wisconsin want to go after MTV when *they* are the ones responsible for the massive failure of American education. Walk into any public school, and the odds are good that you'll find overflowing classrooms, leaking ceilings, and demoralized teachers. In 1 out of 4 schools, you'll find students 'learning' from textbooks published in the 1980s – or earlier.

Why is this? Because the political leaders – and the people who vote for them – have decided it's a bigger priority to build another bomber than to educate our children. They would rather hold hearings about the depravity of a television show called *Jack-ass* than about their own depravity in neglecting our schools and children and maintaining our title as Dumbest Country on Earth.

I hate writing these words. I *love* this big lug of a country and the crazy people in it. But when I can travel to some backwater village in Central America, as I did back in the eighties, and listen to a bunch of twelve-year-olds tell me their concerns about the World Bank, I get the feeling that *something* is lacking in the United States of America.

Our problem isn't that our kids don't know

```
┌─────── PRESIDENTIAL CLIP 'N' CARRY ───────┐
```

List of Leaders of Fifty Largest Countries
(in order of country populations, as of early 2004)

1. CHINA
President Hu Jintao

2. INDIA
Prime Minister Atal Bihari Vajpayee

3. UNITED STATES
'President' George W. Bush

4. INDONESIA
President Megawati Sukarnoputri

5. BRAZIL
President Luiz Inacio Lula da Silva

6. PAKISTAN
chief of state: President Pervez Musharraf

7. RUSSIA
President Vladimir Vladimirovich Putin

8. BANGLADESH
Prime Minister Khaleda Zia

9. NIGERIA
President Olusegun Obasanjo

10. JAPAN
Prime Minister Junichiro Koizumi

11. MEXICO
President Vicente Fox

12. PHILIPPINES
President Gloria Macapagal-Arroyo

13. GERMANY
Chancellor Gerhard Schroeder

14. VIETNAM
President Tran Duc Luong

15. EGYPT
President Mohammed Hosni Mubarak

16. IRAN
Supreme Leader Ayatollah Ali Hoseini-Khamenei

17. TURKEY
chief of state: President Ahmet Necdet Sezer

18. ETHIOPIA
Prime Minister Meles Zenawi

19. THAILAND
Prime Minister Thaksin Chinnawat

20. FRANCE
President Jacques Chirac

21. UNITED KINGDOM
Prime Minister Tony Blair

22. ITALY
Prime Minister Silvio Berlusconi

23. THE DEMOCRATIC REPUBLIC OF CONGO
President Joseph Kabila

24. SOUTH KOREA
President Roh Moo-hyun

25. UKRAINE
President Leonid D. Kuchma

26. SOUTH AFRICA
President Thabo Mbeki

27. BURMA
General Than Shwe

28. COLOMBIA
President Alvaro Uribe Velez

continued

List of Leaders of Fifty Largest Countries
(in order of country populations, as of early 2004)

29. SPAIN
Prime Minister Jose Luis Rodriguez Zapatero

30. ARGENTINA
President Nestor Kirchner

31. POLAND
President Aleksander Kwasniewski

32. SUDAN
President Lt. Gen. Umar Hassan Ahmad al-Bashir

33. TANZANIA
President Benjamin William Mkapa

34. ALGERIA
President Abdelaziz BouteXika

35. CANADA
Prime Minister Paul Martin

36. MOROCCO
Prime Minister Driss Jettou

37. KENYA
President Mawai Kibaki

38. AFGHANISTAN
President Hamid Karzai

39. PERU
President Alejandro Toledo Manrique

40. NEPAL
King Gyanendra Bir Bikram Shah

41. UZBEKISTAN
President Islom Karimov

42. UGANDA
President Lt. Gen. Yoweri Kaguta Museveni

43. IRAQ
'President' George W. Bush

44. VENEZUELA
President Hugo Chavez Frias

45. SAUDI ARABIA
King Fahd bin Abd al-Aziz Al Saud

46. MALAYSIA
Prime Minister Abdullah bin Ahmad Badawi

47. TAIWAN
President Chen Shui-bian

48. NORTH KOREA
Chairman Kim Jong Il

49. ROMANIA
President Ion Iliescu

50. GHANA
President John Agyekum Kufuor

Although it may seem like Australia belongs on this list, it doesn't. Ghana, at #50, has a population of 20,467,747 (2003), while Australia – at #52, behind Sri Lanka – has a population of 19,731,984 (2003). Australia's prime minister is the Bush-brownnoser John Howard.

anything but that the adults who pay their tuition are no better. I wonder what would happen if we tested the U.S. Congress to see just how much our representatives know. What if we were to give a pop quiz to the commentators who cram our TVs and radios with all their nonstop nonsense? How many would *they* get right?

A while back, I decided to find out. It was one of those Sunday mornings when the choice on TV was the *Parade of Homes* real estate show or *The McLaughlin Group*. If you like the sound of hyenas on Dexedrine, of course, you go with *McLaughlin*. On this particular Sunday morning, perhaps as my punishment for not being at Mass, I was forced to listen to magazine columnist Fred Barnes (now an editor at the right-wing *Weekly Standard* and co-host of the Fox News show *The Beltway Boys*) whine on and on about the sorry state of American education, blaming the teachers and their evil union for why students are doing so poorly.

'These kids don't even know what *The Iliad* and *The Odyssey* are!' he bellowed, as the other panelists nodded in admiration at Fred's noble lament.

The next morning I called Fred Barnes at his Washington office. 'Fred,' I said, 'tell me what *The Iliad* and *The Odyssey* are.'

He started hemming and hawing. 'Well, they're . . . uh . . . you know . . . uh . . . okay, fine, you got me – I don't know what they're about. Happy now?'

No, not really. You're one of the top TV pundits in America, seen every week on your own show and plenty of others. You gladly hawk your 'wisdom' to hundreds of thousands of unsuspecting citizens, gleefully scorning others for their ignorance. Yet you and your guests know little or nothing yourselves. Grow up, get some books, and go to your room.

Yale and Harvard. Princeton and Dartmouth. Stanford and Berkeley. Get a degree from one of those universities, and you're set for life. So what if, on that test of the college seniors I previously mentioned, 70 percent of the students at those fine schools had never heard of the Voting Rights Act or President Lyndon Johnson's Great Society initiatives? Who needs to know stuff like that as you sit in your Tuscan villa watching the sunset and checking how well your portfolio did today?

So what if *not one* of these top universities that the ignorant students attend requires that they take even one course in American history to graduate? Who needs history when you are going to be tomorrow's master of the universe?

Who cares if 70 percent of those who graduate from America's colleges are not required to learn a foreign language? Isn't the rest of the world speaking English now? And if they aren't, shouldn't all those damn foreigners GET WITH THE PROGRAM?

And who gives a rat's ass if, out of the seventy English Literature programs at seventy major American universities, only twenty-three now require English majors to take a course in Shakespeare? Can somebody please explain to me what Shakespeare and English have to do with each other? What good are some moldy old plays going to be in the business world, anyway?

Maybe I'm just jealous because I don't have a college degree. Yes, I, Michael Moore, am a college dropout.

Well, I never *officially* dropped out. One day in my sophomore year, I drove around and around the various parking lots of our commuter campus in Flint, searching desperately for a parking space. There simply was no place to park – every spot was full, and no one was leaving. After a frustrating hour spent circling around in my '69 Chevy Impala, I shouted out the window, 'That's it, I'm dropping out!' I drove home and told my parents I was no longer in college.

'Why?' they asked.

'Couldn't find a parking spot,' I replied, grabbing a Redpop and moving on with the rest of my life. I haven't sat at a school desk since.

Important Dates in History

June 19, 1865: 'Juneteenth.' Although the Emancipation Proclamation had pronounced the slaves of the Confederacy free more than two years earlier, the word hadn't gotten to everyone in the South. On this day in Galveston, Texas, a Union general arrived and officially informed the slaves of their freedom.

December 29, 1890: Massacre at Wounded Knee. As part of one last effort to quell the one remaining Indian rebellion, U.S. troops were sent out to arrest Big Foot, the chief of the Sioux Indian tribe. Members of the tribe were captured, forced to give up their arms, and moved into a camp surrounded by the U.S. troops. On the morning of December 29, the soldiers opened fire on the Indian camp and three hundred mostly unarmed Sioux, including Big Foot, were killed. It was the last battle in the four-hundred-year campaign of genocide against the Native Americans.

May 18, 1896: In *Plessy* v. *Ferguson*, the U.S. Supreme Court decided that inferior accommodations for blacks on railroad cars did not constitute a violation of the equal protection clause of the Fourteenth Amendment. The decision paved the way for the 'separate but equal' policies that resulted in Jim Crow laws.

April 14, 1914: The Ludlow Massacre. Colorado coal miners who had been trying for years to unionize went on strike. After being kicked out of their company-owned homes, the strikers and their families set up tent colonies on public property. On the morning of April 14, Colorado militiamen and other strikebreakers fired their guns into the camp and burned down the tents, killing twenty—mostly women and children.

March 22, 1947: President Truman issued Executive Order 9835 to identify the 'infiltration of disloyal persons' within the government. This ushered in an era of fear and paranoia about alleged Communists that led to more than six million people being investigated and five hundred being dismissed from their jobs for 'questionable loyalty.'

December 1, 1955: A tired seamstress and local civil rights activist in Montgomery, Alabama, Rosa Parks, refused to give up her seat on a bus to a white passenger. This quiet act launched the Montgomery bus boycott, which lasted for 381 days and established Martin Luther King Jr. as the movement's leader. The boycott was ended after the Supreme Court ruled that segregation laws on public transportation were illegal.

April 30, 1975: The fall of Saigon. Although American ground troops had officially pulled out of Vietnam two years earlier, this day represents the end of the brutal war. Several weeks of chaos over the impending Communist takeover culminated in a desperate scene as the last of the U.S. rescue helicopters took off from the American embassy's rooftop with the few refugees they could carry.

My dislike of school started somewhere around the second month of first grade. My parents – and God Bless Them Forever for doing this – had taught me to read and write by the time I was four. So when I entered St. John's Elementary School, I had to sit and feign interest while the other kids, like robots, sang, 'A-B-C-D-E-F-G . . . Now I know my ABCs, tell me what you think of me!' Every time I heard that line, I wanted to scream out, 'Here's what I think of you – quit singing that damn song! Somebody get me a Twinkie!'

I was bored beyond belief. The nuns, to their credit, recognized this, and one day Sister John Catherine took me aside and said that they had decided to skip me up to second grade, effective immediately. I was thrilled. When I got home I excitedly announced to my parents that I had already advanced a grade in my first month of school. They seemed underwhelmed by this new evidence of my genius. Instead they let out a 'WHAT THE—,' then went into the kitchen and closed the door. I could hear my mother on the phone explaining to the Mother Superior that there was *no way* her little Michael was going to be attending class with kids bigger and older than him, so please, Sister, put him back in first grade.

I was crushed. My mother explained to me that if I skipped first grade I'd always be the youngest and littlest kid in class all through my school years (well, inertia and fast food eventually proved her wrong on that count). There would be no appeals to my father, who left most education decisions to my mother, the valedictorian of her high school class. I tried to explain that if I was sent back to first grade it would appear that I'd *flunked* second grade on my first day – putting myself at risk of having the crap beaten out of me by the first graders I'd left behind with a rousing 'See ya, suckers!' But Mom wasn't falling for it; it was then I learned that the only person with higher authority than Mother Superior was Mother Moore.

The next day I decided to ignore all instructions from my parents to go back to first grade. In the morning, before the opening bell, all the students had to line up outside the school with their classmates and then march into the building in single file. Quietly, but defiantly, I went and stood in the second graders' line, praying that God would strike the nuns blind so they wouldn't see which line I was in. The bell rang – and no one had spotted me! The second grade line started to move, and I went with it. *Yes!* I thought. *If I can pull this off, if I can just get into that second grade classroom and take my seat, then nobody will be able to get me out of there.* Just as I was about to enter the door of the school, I felt a hand grab me by the collar of my coat. It was Sister John Catherine.

'I think you're in the wrong line, Michael,' she said firmly. 'You are now in first grade again.' I began to protest: my parents had it 'all wrong,' or 'those weren't *really* my parents,' or . . .

For the next twelve years I sat in class, did my work, and remained constantly preoccupied, looking for ways to bust out. I started an underground school paper in fourth grade. It was shut down. I started it again in sixth. It was shut down. In eighth grade I not only started the paper again, I convinced the good sisters to let me write a play for our class to perform at the Christmas pageant. The play had something to do with how many rats occupied the parish hall and how all the rats in the country had descended on St. John's Parish Hall to have their annual 'rat convention.' The priest put a stop to that one – and shut down the paper again. Instead, my friends and I were told to go up on stage and sing three Christmas carols and then leave the stage without uttering a word. I organized half the class to go up there and utter nothing. So we stood there and refused to sing the carols, our silent protest against censorship. By the second song, intimidated by the stern looks from their parents in the audience, most of the protesters joined in on the singing – and by the third song, I, too, had capitulated, joining in on 'O Holy Night,' and promising myself to live to fight another day.

High school, as we all know, is some sort of sick, sadistic punishment of kids by adults seeking vengeance because they can no longer lead the responsibility-free, screwing-around-24/7 lives young people enjoy. What other explanation could there be for those four brutal years of degrading comments, physical abuse, and the belief that you're the only one not having sex?

As soon as I entered high school – and the public school system – all the grousing I'd done about the repression of the Sisters of St. Joseph was forgotten; suddenly they all looked like scholars and saints. I was now walking the halls of a two-thousand-plus-inmate holding pen. Where the nuns had devoted their lives to teaching for no earthly reward, those running the public high school had one simple mission: 'Hunt these little pricks down like dogs, then cage them until we can either break their will or ship them off to the glue factory!' Do this, don't do that, tuck your shirt in, wipe that smile off your face, where's your hall pass, THAT'S THE WRONG PASS! *YOU – DETENTION!!*

One day I came home from school and picked up the paper. The headline read: '26th Amendment Passes – Voting Age Lowered to 18.' Below that was another headline: 'School Board President to Retire, Seat Up for Election.'

Hmm. I called the county clerk.

'Uh, I'm gonna be eighteen in a few weeks. If I can vote, does that I mean I can also run for office?'

'Let me see,' the lady replied. 'That's a new question!'

Guide to Student Rights

As an American student you probably haven't learned much about the U.S. constitution or about your civil rights, so here's a handy guide based on information from the American Civil Liberties Union (ACLU). For more facts about student rights, on subjects including dress codes, your school records, and discrimination based on sexual orientation, contact your state chapter of the ACLU or check their Web site at www.aclu.org/StudentsRights/ StudentsRightsMain.cfm

- The First Amendment to the Constitution guarantees the right to free expression and free association. And according to the United States Supreme Court, these rights even apply to you, the lowly student – at least some of the time.

- In 1969, the Supreme Court (in *Tinker* v. *Des Moines Independent Community School District*) ruled that the First Amendment applies to students in public schools. Private schools have more leeway to set their own rules on free expression because they are not operated by the government.

• Public school students can express their opinions orally and in writing (in leaflets or on buttons, armbands or T-shirts), as long as they do not 'materially and substantially' disrupt classes or other school activities.

• School officials can probably prohibit students from using 'vulgar or indecent language,' but they cannot censor only one side of a controversy.

• If you and other students produce your own newspaper and want to hand it out in school, administrators cannot censor you or prohibit distribution of the paper (unless it is 'indecent' or handing it out disrupts school activities).

• But administrators *can* censor what appears in the official school paper (the one that is published with school money). In the 1988 decision *Hazelwood School District* v. *Kuhlmeier*, the United States Supreme Court held that public school administrators can censor student speech in official school publications or activities (like a school play, art exhibit, yearbook, or newspaper) if the officials think students are saying something inappropriate or harmful – even if it is not vulgar and does not disrupt activity.

- Some states – including Colorado, California, Iowa, Kansas, and Massachusetts – have "High School Free Expression" laws that give students expanded free speech rights. Check with your local ACLU to find out if your state has such laws.

She ruffled through some papers and came back on the phone. 'Yes,' she said, 'you can run. All you need to do is gather twenty signatures to place your name on the ballot.'

Twenty signatures? That's it? I had no idea running for elective office required so little work. I got the twenty signatures, submitted my petition, and started campaigning. My platform? 'Fire the high school principal and the assistant principal!'

Alarmed at the idea that a high school student

might actually find a legal means to remove the very administrators he was being paddled by, five local 'adults' took out petitions and got themselves added to the ballot, too.

Of course, they ended up splitting the older adult vote five ways – and I won, getting the vote of every single stoner between the ages of eighteen and twenty-five (who, though many would probably never vote again, relished the thought of sending their high school wardens to the gallows).

The day after I won, I was walking down the hall at school (I had one more week to serve out as a student), and I passed the assistant principal, my shirt tail proudly untucked.

'Good morning, Mr. Moore,' he said tersely. The day before, my name had been 'Hey-You!' Now I was his boss.

Within nine months after I took my seat on the school board, the principal and assistant principal had submitted their 'letters of resignation,' a face-saving device employed when one is 'asked' to step down. A couple of years later the principal suffered a heart attack and died.

I had known this man, the principal, for many years. When I was eight years old, he used to let me and my friends skate and play hockey on this little pond beside his house. He was kind and generous, and always left the door to his house open in case any of us needed to change into our skates or if we got cold and just wanted to get warm. Years later, I was asked to play bass in a band that was forming, but I didn't own a bass. He let me borrow his son's.

I offer this to remind myself that all people are actually good at their core, and to remember that someone with whom I grew to have serious disputes was also someone with a free cup of hot chocolate for us shivering little brats from the neighborhood.

Teachers are now the politicians' favorite punching bag. To listen to the likes of Chester Finn, a former assistant secretary of education in Bush the Elder's administration, you'd think all that has crumbled in our society can be traced back to lax, lazy, and incompetent teachers. 'If you put out a Ten-Most-Wanted list of who's killing American education, I'm not sure who you would have higher on the list: the teachers' union or the education school faculties,' Finn said.

Sure, there are a lot of teachers who suck, and they'd be better suited to making telemarketing calls for Amway. But the vast majority are dedicated educators who have chosen a profession that pays them less than what some of their students earn selling Ecstasy, and for that sacrifice we seek to punish them. I don't know about you, but I want the people who have the direct attention of my child more hours a day than I do treated with tender loving care. Those are my kids they're 'preparing' for this world, so why on earth would I want to piss them off?

You would think society's attitude would be something like this:

Teachers, thank you so much for devoting your life to my child. Is there ANYTHING I can do to help you? Is there ANYTHING you need? I am here for you. Why? Because you are helping my child – MY BABY – learn and grow. Not only will you be largely responsible for her ability to make a living, but your influence will greatly affect how she views the world, what she knows about other people in this world, and how she will feel about herself. I want her to believe she can attempt anything – that no doors are closed and that no dreams are too distant. I am entrusting the most valuable person in my life to you for seven hours each day. You are, thus, one of the most important people in my life! Thank you.

No, instead, this is what teachers hear:

'You've got to wonder about teachers who claim to put the interests of children first – and then look to milk the system dry through wage hikes.' (*New York Post*, 12/26/00)

'Estimates of the number of bad teachers range from 5 percent to 18 percent of the 2.6 million total.' (Michael Chapman, *Investor's Business Daily*, 9/21/98)

'Most education professionals belong to a closed community of devotees . . . who follow popular philosophies rather than research on what works.' (Douglas Carminen, quoted in the *Montreal Gazette*, 1/6/01)

'Teachers unions have gone to bat for felons and teachers who have had sex with students, as well as those who simply couldn't teach.' (Peter Schweizen, *National Review*, 8/17/98)

What kind of priority do we place on education in America? Oh, it's on the funding list – somewhere down between OSHA and meat inspectors. The person who cares for our child every day receives an average of $41,351 annually. A Congressman who cares only about which tobacco lobbyist is taking him to dinner tonight receives $145,100.

Considering the face-slapping society gives our teachers on a daily basis, is it any wonder so few choose the profession? The national teacher shortage is so big that some school systems are recruiting teachers outside the United States. Chicago recently recruited and hired teachers from twenty-eight foreign countries, including China, France, and Hungary. By the time the new term began in New York City, seven thousand veteran teachers had retired – and 60 percent of the new teachers hired to replace them were uncertified.

But here's the kicker for me: 163 New York City schools opened the 2000–2001 school year *without a principal*! You heard right – school, with *no one in charge*. Apparently the mayor and the school board were experimenting with chaos theory – throw five hundred poor kids into a crumbling building, and watch nature take its course! In the city from which most of the wealth in the world is controlled, where there are more millionaires per square foot than there is gum on the sidewalk, we somehow can't find the money to pay a starting teacher more than $31,900 a year. And we act surprised when we can't get results.

And it's not just teachers who have been neglected – American schools are *literally* falling apart. In 1999 one-quarter of U.S. public schools reported that the condition of at least one of their buildings was inadequate. In 1997 the entire Washington, D.C., school system had to delay the start of school for three weeks because nearly *one-third* of the schools were found to be unsafe.

Almost 10 percent of U.S. public schools have

enrollments that are more than 25 percent greater than the capacity of their permanent buildings. Classes have to be held in the hallways, outdoors, in the gym, in the cafeteria; one school I visited even held classes in a janitor's closet. It's not as if the janitors' closets are being used for anything related to cleaning, anyway – in New York City almost 15 percent of the eleven hundred public schools are without full-time custodians, forcing teachers to mop their own floors and students to do without toilet paper. We already send our kids out into the street to hawk candy bars so their schools can buy band instruments – what's next? Car washes to raise money for toilet paper?

Further proof of just how special our little offspring are is the number of public and even school libraries that have been shut down or had their hours cut back. The last thing we need is a bunch of kids hanging out around a bunch of books!

Apparently 'President' Bush agreed: in his first budget he proposed cutting federal spending on libraries by $39 million, down to $168 million – a nearly 19 percent reduction. Just the week before, his wife, former school librarian Laura Bush, kicked off a national campaign for America's libraries, calling them 'community treasure chests, loaded with a wealth of information available to everyone, equally.' The President's mother, Barbara Bush, heads the Foundation for Family Literacy. Well, there's nothing like having firsthand experience with illiteracy in the family to motivate one into acts of charity.

For kids who are exposed to books at home, the loss of a library is sad. But for kids who come from environments where people don't read, the loss of a library is a tragedy that might keep them from ever discovering the joys of reading – or from gathering the kind of information that will decide their lot in life. Jonathan Kozol, for decades an advocate for disadvantaged children, has observed that school libraries 'remain the clearest window to a world of noncommercial satisfactions and enticements that most children in poor neighborhoods will ever know.'

Kids deprived of access to good libraries are also being kept from developing the information skills they need to keep up in workplaces that are increasingly dependent on rapidly changing information. The ability to conduct research is 'probably the most essential skill [today's students] can have,' says Julie Walker, executive director of the American Association of School Librarians. 'The knowledge [students] acquire in school is not going to serve them throughout their lifetimes. Many of them will have four to five careers in a lifetime. It will be their ability to navigate information that will matter.'

Who's to blame for the decline in libraries? Well, when it comes to school libraries, you can start by pointing the finger (yes, *that* finger) at Richard Nixon. From the 1960s until 1974, school libraries received specific funding from the government. But in 1974 the Nixon administration changed the rules, stipulating that federal education money be doled out in 'block grants' to be spent by states however they chose. Few states chose to spend the money on libraries, and the downslide began. This is one reason that materials in many school libraries today date from the 1960s and early 1970s, before funding was diverted. ('No, Sally, the Soviet Union isn't our enemy. The Soviet Union has been kaput for ten years. . . .')

This 1999 account by an *Education Week* reporter about the 'library' at a Philadelphia elementary school could apply to any number of similarly neglected schools:

Even the best books in the library at T. M. Pierce Elementary School are dated, tattered, and discolored. The worst – many in a latter stage of disintegration – are dirty and fetid and leave a moldy residue on hands and clothing. Chairs and tables are old, mismatched, or broken. There isn't a computer in sight. . . . Outdated facts and theories and offensive stereotypes leap from the authoritative pages of encyclopedias and biographies, fiction and nonfiction tomes. Among the volumes on these shelves a student would find it all but impossible to locate accurate information on AIDS or other contemporary diseases, explorations of the moon and Mars, or the past five U.S. presidents.

The ultimate irony in all of this is that the very politicians who refuse to fund education in America adequately are the same ones who go ballistic over how our kids have fallen behind the Germans, the Japanese, and just about every other country with running water and an economy not based on the sale of Chiclets. Suddenly they want 'accountability.' They want the teachers held responsible and to be tested. And they want the kids to be tested – over and over and over.

There's nothing terribly wrong with the concept of using standardized testing to determine whether kids are learning to read and write and do math. But too many politicians and education bureaucrats have created a national obsession with testing, as if everything that's wrong with the educational system in this country would be magically fixed if we could just raise those scores.

The people who really should be tested (besides the yammering pundits) are the so-called political leaders. Next time you see your state representative or congressman, give him this pop quiz – and remind him that any future pay raises will be based on how well he scores:

1. What is the annual pay of your average constituent?

2. What percent of welfare recipients are children?

3. How many known species of plants and animals are on the brink of extinction?

4. How big is the hole in the ozone layer?

5. Which African countries have a lower infant mortality rate than Detroit?

6. How many American cities still have two competing newspapers?

7. How many ounces in a gallon?

8. Which do I stand a greater chance of being killed by: a gun shot in school or a bolt of lightning?

9. What's the only state capital without a McDonald's?

10. Describe the story of either *The Iliad* or *The Odyssey*.

Answers

1. $28,548

2. 67 percent

3. 11,046

4. 10.5 million square miles

5. Libya, Mauritius, Seychelles

6. 34

7. 128 ounces

8. You're twice as likely to be killed by lightning as by a gun-shot in school.

9. Montpelier, Vermont.

10. *The Iliad* is an ancient Greek epic poem by Homer about the Trojan War. *The Odyssey* is another epic poem by Homer recounting the ten-year journey home from the Trojan War made by Odysseus, the king of Ithaca.

Chances are, the genius representing you in the legislature won't score 50 percent on the above test. The good news is that you get to flunk him within a year or two.

*

There is one group in the country that isn't just sitting around carping about all them lamebrain teachers – a group that cares deeply about what kinds of students will enter the adult world. You could say they have a vested interest in this captive audience of millions of young people . . . or in the billions of dollars they spend each year. (Teenagers alone spent more than $150 billion last year.) Yes, it's Corporate America, whose generosity to our nation's schools is just one more example of their continuing patriotic service.

Just how committed are these companies to our children's schools?

According to numbers collected by the Center for the Analysis of Commercialism in Education (CACE), their selfless charity has seen a tremendous boom since 1990. Over the past ten years, school programs and activities have seen corporate sponsorship increase by 248 percent. In exchange for this sponsorship, schools allow the corporation to associate its name with the events.

For example, Eddie Bauer sponsors the final round of the National Geography Bee. Book covers featuring Calvin Klein and Nike ads are distributed to students. Nike and other shoemakers, looking for early access to tomorrow's stars, sponsor inner-city high school basketball teams.

Pizza Hut set up its 'Book-It!' program to encourage children to read. When students meet the monthly reading goal, they are rewarded with a certificate for a Pizza Hut personal pan pizza. At the restaurant, the store manager personally congratulates the children and gives them each a sticker and a certificate. Pizza Hut suggests school principals place a 'Pizza Hut Book-It!' honor roll list in the school for everyone to see.

General Mills and Campbell's Soup thought up a better plan. Instead of giving free rewards, they both have programs rewarding schools for getting parents to buy their products. Under General Mills's 'Box Tops for Education' program, schools get ten cents for each box top logo they send in, and can earn up to $10,000 a year. That's 100,000 General Mills products sold. Campbell's Soup's 'Labels for Education' program is no better. It touts itself as 'Providing America's children with FREE school equipment!' Schools can earn one 'free' Apple iMac computer for only 94,950 soup labels. Campbell's suggests setting a goal of a label a day from each student. Based on that conservative estimate of five labels per week per child, an over-crowded, under-privileged class of thirty kids could get that 'free' computer in just 633 weeks.

It's not just this kind of sponsorship that brings these schools and corporations together. The 1990s saw a phenomenal 1,384 percent increase in exclusive agreements between schools and soft-drink bottlers. Two hundred and forty school districts in thirty-one states have sold exclusive rights to one of the big three soda companies (Coca-Cola, Pepsi, Dr. Pepper) to push their products in schools. Anybody wonder why there are more overweight kids than ever before? Or more young women with calcium deficiencies because they're drinking less milk? And even though federal law prohibits the sale of soft drinks in schools until lunch periods begin, in some overcrowded schools 'lunch' begins in midmorning. Artificially flavored carbonated sugar water – the breakfast of champions! In March 2001 Coke responded to public pressure, announcing that it would add water, juice, and other sugar-free, caffeine-free, and calcium-rich alternatives to soda to its school vending machines.

I guess they can afford such concessions when you consider their deal with the Colorado Springs school district. Colorado has been a trailblazer when it comes to tie-ins between the schools and soft drink companies. In Colorado Springs, the district will receive $8.4 million over ten years from its deal with Coca-Cola – and more if it exceeds its 'requirement' of selling seventy thousand cases of Coke products a year. To ensure the levels are met, school district officials urged principals to allow students unlimited access to Coke machines and allow students to drink Coke in the classroom.

But Coke isn't alone. In the Jefferson County, Colorado, school district (home of Columbine High School), Pepsi contributed $1.5 million to help build a new sports stadium. Some county schools tested a science course, developed in part by Pepsi, called 'The Carbonated Beverage Company.' Students taste-tested colas, analyzed cola samples, watched a video tour of a Pepsi bottling plant, and visited a local plant.

The school district in Wylie, Texas, signed a deal in 1996 that shared the rights to sell soft drinks in the schools between Coke and Dr. Pepper. Each company paid $31,000 a year. Then, in 1998, the county changed its mind and signed a deal with Coke worth $1.2 million over fifteen years. Dr. Pepper sued the county for breach of contract. The school district bought out Dr. Pepper's contract, costing them $160,000 – plus another $20,000 in legal fees.

It's not just the companies that sometimes get sent packing. Students who lack the proper corporate school spirit do so at considerable risk. When Mike Cameron wore a Pepsi shirt on 'Coke Day' at Greenbrier High School in Evans, Georgia, he was suspended for a day. 'Coke Day' was part of the school's entry in a national 'Team Up With

Coca-Cola' contest, which awards $10,000 to the high school that comes up with the best plan for distributing Coke discount cards. Greenbrier school officials said Cameron was suspended for 'being disruptive and trying to destroy the school picture' when he removed an outer shirt and revealed the Pepsi shirt as a photograph was being taken of students posed to spell out the word *Coke*. Cameron said the shirt was visible all day, but he didn't get in trouble until posing for the picture. No slouch in the marketing department, Pepsi quickly sent the high school senior a box of Pepsi shirts and hats.

If turning the students into billboards isn't enough, schools and corporations sometimes turn the school itself into one giant neon sign for corporate America. Appropriation of school space, including scoreboards, rooftops, walls, and text-books, for corporate logos and advertising is up 539 percent.

Colorado Springs, not satisfied to sell its soul only to Coca-Cola, has plastered its school buses with advertisements for Burger King, Wendy's, and other big companies. Free book covers and school planners with ads for Kellogg's Pop-Tarts and pictures of FOX TV personalities were also handed out to the students.

After members of the Grapevine-Colleyville

Independent School District in Texas decided they
didn't want advertisements in the classrooms, they
allowed Dr. Pepper and 7-Up logos to be painted
on the rooftops of two high schools. The two high
schools, not coincidentally, lie under the Dallas
airport flight path.

The schools aren't just looking for ways to advertise; they're also concerned with the students'
perceptions of various products. That's why, in
some schools, companies conduct market research
in classrooms during school hours. Education
Market Resources of Kansas reports that 'children
respond openly and easily to questions and stim-
uli' in the classroom setting. Of course, that's what
they're *supposed* to be doing in a classroom – but
for their own benefit, not that of some corporate
pollsters. Filling out marketing surveys instead of
learning, however, is probably *not* what they should
be doing.

Companies have also learned they can reach this
confined audience by 'sponsoring' educational materials. This practice, like the others, has exploded as
well, increasing 1,875 percent since 1990.

Teachers have shown a Shell Oil video that
teaches students that the way to experience nature
is by driving there – after filling your Jeep's gas tank
at a Shell station. ExxonMobil prepared lesson
plans about the flourishing wildlife in Prince

William Sound, site of the ecological disaster caused by the oil spill from the Exxon Valdez. A third-grade math book features exercises involving counting Tootsie Rolls. A Hershey's-sponsored curriculum used in many schools features 'The Chocolate Dream Machine,' including lessons in math, science, geography – and nutrition.

In a number of high schools, the economics course is supplied by General Motors. GM writes and provides the textbooks and the course outline. Students learn from GM's example the benefits of capitalism and how to operate a company – like GM.

And what better way to imprint a corporate logo on the country's children than through television and the Internet beamed directly into the classroom. Electronic marketing, where a company provides programming or equipment to schools for the right to advertise to their students, is up 139 percent.

One example is the ZapMe! Corporation, which provides schools with a free computer lab and access to pre-selected Web sites. In return, schools must promise that the lab will be in use at least four hours a day. The catch? The ZapMe! Web browser has constantly scrolling advertisements – and the company gets to collect information on students' browsing habits, information they can then sell to other companies.

Perhaps the worst of the electronic marketers is Channel One Television. Eight million students in 12,000 classrooms watch Channel One, an in-school news *and advertising* program, every day. (That's right: EVERY day.) Kids are spending the equivalent of six full school days a year watching Channel One in almost 40 percent of U.S. middle and high schools. Instructional time lost to the ads alone? One entire day per year. That translates into an annual cost to taxpayers of more than $1.8 billion.

Sure, doctors and educators agree that our kids can never watch enough TV. And there's probably a place in school for some television programs – I have fond memories of watching astronauts blasting off on the television rolled into my grade school auditorium. But out of the daily twelve-minute Channel One broadcasts, only 20 percent of the airtime is devoted to stories about politics, the economy, and cultural and social issues. That leaves a whopping 80 percent for advertising, sports, weather, features, and Channel One promotions.

Channel One is disproportionately shown in schools in low income communities with large minority populations, where the least money is available for education, and where the least amount is spent on textbooks and other academic materials. Once these districts receive corporate handouts, government's failure to provide adequate school funding tends to remain unaddressed.

For most of us, the only time we enter an

Are You a Potential School Shooter?

The following is a list of traits the FBI has identified as 'risk factors' among students who may commit violent acts. Stay away from any student showing signs of:

- Poor coping skills
- Access to weapons
- Depression
- Drug and alcohol abuse
- Alienation
- Narcissism
- Inappropriate humor
- Unlimited, unmonitored television and Internet use

Since this includes all of you, drop out of school immediately. Home schooling is not a viable option, because you must also stay away from yourself.

American high school is to vote at our local precinct. (There's an irony if there ever was one – going to participate in democracy's sacred ritual while two thousand students in the same building live under some sort of totalitarian dictatorship.) The halls are packed with burned-out teenagers shuffling from class to class, dazed and confused, wondering what the hell they're doing there. They learn how to regurgitate answers the state wants them to give, and any attempt to be an individual is now grounds for being suspected to be a member of the trench coat mafia. I visited a school recently, and some students asked me if I noticed that they and the other students in the school were all wearing white or some neutral color. Nobody dares wear black, or anything else wild and distinct. That's a sure ticket to the principal's office – where the school psychologist will be waiting to ascertain whether that Limp Bizkit shirt you have on means that you intend to shoot up Miss Nelson's fourth hour geometry class.

So the kids learn to submerge any personal expression. They learn that it's better to go along so that you get along. They learn that to rock the boat could get them rocked right out of the school. Don't question authority. Do as you're told. Don't think, just do as I say.

Oh, and have a good and productive life as an

active, well-adjusted participant in our thriving
democracy!

How to be a Student Subversive instead of a Student Subservient

There are many ways you can fight back at your
high school – and have fun while doing it. The key
thing is to learn what all the rules are, and what
your rights are by law and by school district policy.
This will help to prevent you getting in the kind
of trouble you don't need.

It may also get you some cool perks. David
Schankula, a college student who has helped me
on this book, recalls that when he was in high
school in Kentucky, he and his buddies found some
obscure state law that said any student who
requests a day off to go to the state fair must be
given the day off. The state legislature probably
passed this law years ago to help some farm kid
take his prize hog to the fair without being penal-
ized at school. But the law was still on the books,
and it gave any student the right to request the
state fair day off – regardless of the reason. So you
can imagine the look on the principal's face when
David and his city friends submitted their request

for their free day off from school – and there was nothing the principal could do.

Here's a few more things you can do:

I. MOCK THE VOTE.

Student council and class elections are the biggest smokescreen the school throws up, fostering the illusion that you actually have any say in the running of the school. Most students who run for these offices either take the charade too seriously – or they just think it'll look good on their college applications.

So why not run yourself? Run just to ridicule the whole ridiculous exercise. Form your own party, with its own stupid name. Campaign on wild promises: *If elected, I'll change the school mascot to an amoeba*, or *If elected, I'll insist that the principal must first eat the school lunch each day before it is fed to the students*. Put up banners with cool slogans: 'Vote for me – a real loser!'

If you get elected, you can devote your energies to accomplishing things that will drive the administration crazy, but help out your fellow students (demands for free condoms, student evaluations of teachers, less homework so you can get to bed by midnight, etc.).

2. START A SCHOOL CLUB.

You have a right to do this. Find a sympathetic teacher to sponsor it. The Pro-Choice Club. The Free Speech Club. The Integrate Our Town Club. Make every member a 'president' of the club, so they all can claim it on their college applications. One student I know tried to start a Feminist Club, but the principal wouldn't allow it because then they'd be obliged to give equal time to a Male Chauvinist Club. That's the kind of idiot thinking you'll encounter, but don't give up. (Heck, if you find yourself in that situation, just say *fine* – and suggest that the principal could sponsor the Chauvinist Club.)

3. LAUNCH YOUR OWN NEWSPAPER OR WEBZINE.

You have a constitutionally protected right to do this. If you take care not to be obscene, or libelous, or give them any reason to shut you down, this can be a great way to get the truth out about what's happening at your school. Use humor. The students will love it.

4. GET INVOLVED IN THE COMMUNITY.

Go to the school board meetings and inform them what's going on in the school. Petition them to change things. They will try to ignore you or make you sit through a long, boring meeting before they let you speak, but they have to let you speak. Write letters to the editor of your local paper. Adults don't have a clue about what goes on in your high school. Fill them in. More than likely you'll find someone there who'll support you.

Any or all of this will raise quite a ruckus, but there's help out there if you need it. Contact the local American Civil Liberties Union if the school retaliates. Threaten lawsuits – school administrators HATE to hear that word. Just remember: there's no greater satisfaction than seeing the look on your principal's face when you have the upper hand. Use it.

And Never Forget This:

There Is No Permanent Record!

The People's Prayer

I think it was Thomas Aquinas who once observed, 'There's nothing like your own shit to make you realize how much you stink.'

In July 2001, Nancy Reagan, then keeping a round-the-clock watch at her husband's deathbed, dispatched former Reagan henchmen Michael Deaver and Kenneth Duberstein to Washington, D.C., with a private message to George W. Bush and the Republican leadership. The party had been divided over the issue of stem cell research, the ongoing science of taking stem cells from discarded human embryos and using those cells to treat people with debilitating conditions like Alzheimer's (the affliction that had visited former President Reagan), or find cures for other life-threatening diseases. The anti-abortion zealots (among whom are included the Reagans and the Bushes) who have controlled the party for decades demanded that there be no embryonic research, regardless of the suffering of the living.

W. had been leaning toward banning the research, telling the public, in essence, that he saw those dead embryos as living babies. I guess he feared that women would run out and fertilize their eggs just so they could get an embryo, have an abortion, and then sell the embryos for research. Such is the active fantasy life of the conservative nutcases who run this country.

But now the nuts were coming unscrewed, as a number of conservatives, from Tommy Thompson to Connie Mack, were giving their approval to stem cell research, declaring that it had nothing to do with the taking of a 'human life.' Suddenly the media were full of stories of a conservative mutiny on the issue. Right to Life went to war to stop the flood toward reason.

W., though, seemed unfazed and unmoved, more concerned with the brand of toothpaste the British prime minister was using than with changing his antiabortion position.

But then the word came from Nancy. The soon-to-be-widow asked Bush to change his mind and approve, support, fund, and champion stem cell research. The research, she relayed to him through her errand boys, might save Ronnie or future Ronnies suffering from Alzheimer's, Parkinson's, Lou Gehrig's, and other catastrophic illnesses. Nancy had already been modifying her abortion stance over the past few years, and now she was coming out for the first time and saying, no, an embryo is NOT a human being.

In that one moment, the entire playing field
shifted. The call from the front office had been made:
SCREW THE UNBORN! SAVE THE GIPPER!

And sure enough, within days, Baby Bush's principles were disappearing faster than a Condit
intern. Word came from the White House that
now there was nothing wrong with 'certain' stem
cell research. Bush went on TV and would not say
that a human embryo was a *human being*. After
decades of cramming it down our throats that
'human life begins at conception,' we were now
being told by the same individuals who trashed a
woman's right to an abortion that these 'unborn
babies' were actually nothing more than some dead
embryonic tissue – which might just keep some
sick rich people alive a few more years!

All over the country, Republican honchos
joined in the call for more stem cell research.
Orrin Hatch led the charge, saying, 'This is not a
question of the destruction of human life, it's a
question of facilitation of human life.' Even
Strom 'only-in-cases-of-rape-or-incest' Thurmond
agreed. 'Stem cell research could potentially treat
and cure such maladies as multiple sclerosis,
Alzheimer's, Parkinson's, heart disease, various
types of cancer, and diabetes. . . . I am encour-
aged by this pioneering science and support
federal funding for its research,' said the old man,

whose daughter, not so coincidentally, suffers from juvenile diabetes.

There's nothing more lovable than an unembarrassed hypocrite from the Right. They spend their entire lives making everyone else's life miserable, but as soon as a little misery enters their lives, then it's 'Belief system be damned – I want results!' They devote all their energies for years to making it hard for blacks, chicks, or guys who like guys to get ahead or be treated with an ounce of dignity, but the minute someone in *their* family is being held back – whoa, you better get outta my kid's way, buster – he's special!

Reagan, Bush, Cheney, and the whole Lott of them are responsible for decades of cruel legislation designed to punish the poor, imprison those with health problems (drug addictions), or strip rights from desperate people here in America 'illegally.' But when they find *themselves* in a desperate situation, suddenly they have the compassion of St. Francis and the mercy of Mother Theresa.

The rich and powerful make it their mission in life to destroy our air, poison our water, rip us off, and make it impossible for us to get any sort of help at the customer service window, but when their actions come back to haunt *them* they aren't spooked – they're looking for a handout.

Well, I say that's a good thing! Let's hope they

get all they're looking for. If it takes a personal tragedy for them to come to their senses, so be it. After all, in spite of their seven-bathroom houses and garages full of Bentleys, they're just like us. They are H-U-M-A-N. And when a loved one of theirs is lying in bed constantly soiling their adult diapers, pissing all over the new designer sheets, and blabbering on like the crippled souls whose care and funding they just cut from the federal budget – well, in times like these, rich or poor, pus from facial sores all starts looking the same. Equality achieved – one nation, incapacitated, with justice for all.

So now, thanks to Ronald Reagan's misfortune, we're going to get a little federally funded stem cell research – maybe even find a cure for Alzheimer's and God knows what else. Just think about that for a minute. This is what it takes today to get a little responsible scientific research funded. Our beloved former leader, who helped ruin the lives of millions of women because he thought these embryos were little tykes, now finds himself in a debilitating pickle – and just because hordes of conservatives consider him a saint, millions of average Americans will finally be relieved of their suffering?

This phenomenon – the well-heeled changing their tune as soon as they become the victims – is happening everywhere. In New York City, Republican mayor Rudolph Giuliani, who for years opposed the city paying for health care for un-insured children, did an abrupt about-face – after he came down with cancer. 'I have to admit,' a humbled Giuliani explained to the press, 'once I got cancer, I began to see a lot of things in a new light.'

Or take Big Dick Cheney. Cheney quietly halts any antigay initiatives that may come from the White House. Why? Because his daughter is a lesbian. Where would Dick Cheney stand on this issue if a loved one of his weren't gay? Probably not too far down that road in Wyoming where Matthew Shepard was left to die on a cross of fence posts. These faggots and fairies take on a whole new dimension when one of them sprang from your loins. The day his daughter came out of the closet was at least one day Dick Cheney stopped being a fat-cat Republican and responded like a human being and a father. When it hits home, it's very hard to keep acting like an asshole.

So I've decided that the only hope we have in this country to bring aid to the sick, protection to the victims of discrimination, and a better life to those who suffer is to pray like crazy that those in power are afflicted with the worst possible diseases, tragedies, and circumstances in life. Because I can guarantee you, as soon as it's their ass on the line, we're all on the way to being saved.

With that in mind, I've written a prayer to speed the recovery of all those in need, by asking God to smite every political leader and corporate executive with some form of deadly disease. I know it isn't nice to ask God to bring harm to others, but I'd like to think that God is not only merciful and just, he also has a highly developed sense of irony. I think he'd like to see a little grief come to those who have abused his planet and his children.

So I have written 'A Prayer to Afflict the Comfortable with As Many Afflictions As Possible.' After all, history tells us that God enjoys a good old-fashioned smiting every now and then – and who better to smite than the Stupid White types who got us into this mess?

Please pray this prayer with me each morning, preferably before the opening bell of the NYSE. It matters not what religion you claim, or if you claim none at all. This prayer is nondiscriminatory, portable, and requires no collection plate.

Half of Africa will soon be dying of AIDS. Twelve million kids in America today do not get to eat the food they need. Texas is still executing innocent citizens. Time's a-wasting. Bow your heads and join with me now. . . .

A Prayer to Afflict the Comfortable

Dear Lord (God/Yahweh/Buddha/Bob/Nobody):

We beseech You, O merciful One, to bring comfort to those who suffer today for whatever reason You, Nature, or the World Bank has deemed appropriate. We realize, O heavenly Father, that You cannot cure all the sick at once – that would surely empty out the hospitals the good nuns have established in Your name. And we accept that You, the Omniscient One, cannot eliminate all the evil in the world, for that would surely put Thee out of a job.

Rather, dear Lord, we ask that You inflict every member of the House of Representatives with horrible, incurable cancers of the brain, penis, and hand (though not necessarily in that order). We ask, Our Loving Father, that every senator from the South be rendered addicted to drugs and find himself locked away for life. We beseech You to make the children of every senator in the Mountain Time Zone gay – *really* gay. Put the children of senators from the East in a wheelchair and the children of senators from the West in a public school. We implore, Most Merciful One, just as You turned Lot's wife into a pillar of salt, that You turn the rich – *all* the rich – into paupers and homeless, wiping out their entire savings, assets, and mutual funds. Remove from them their positions of power, and yea, may they walk through the valley and into the darkness of a welfare office. Condemn them to a life of flipping burgers and dodging bill collectors. Let them hear the wailing of the innocents as they sit in the middle seat of row 43 in coach and let them feel the gnashing of teeth that are abscessed and rotted like the 108 million who have no dental coverage.

Heavenly Father, we pray that all white leaders (especially the alumni of Bob Jones University) who believe black people have it good these days be risen from their sleep tomorrow morning with their skin as black as a stretch limo so that they may enjoy the riches and reap the bountiful fruits of being black in America. We humbly request that Your anointed ones, the bishops of the Holy Roman Catholic Church, be smitten with ovaries and unplanned pregnancies and a pamphlet about the rhythm method.

Finally, dear Lord, we call upon You to have Jack Welch swim the Hudson he has polluted, to force Hollywood's executives to sit and watch their own movies over and over and over, to have Jesse Helms kissed on the lips by a man of his own gender, to make Chris Matthews go mute, to let the air – quickly – out of Bill O'Reilly, and turn to ash all who are responsible for those who smoke in my office. Oh, yes, and unleash with a fury a plague of locusts to nest in the toupee of Senator Trent Lott from the great state of Mississippi.

May You hear our prayers and grant them, O King of Kings, Who sits on high and watches over us as best You can, considering what screwups we are. Grant us some relief from our misery and suffering, as we know that the men You shall smite will be swift in their efforts to rid themselves of their misfortune, which in turn may rid us of ours.

With this we pray, in the name of the Father, and of the Son, and of the Holy-Spirit-Who-Used-to-Be-a-Ghost, Amen.

POCKET PENGUINS

POCKET PENGUINS

36. **Muriel Spark** The Snobs
37. **Steven Pinker** Hotheads
38. **Tony Harrison** Under the Clock
39. **John Updike** Three Trips
40. **Will Self** Design Faults in the Volvo 760 Turbo
41. **H. G. Wells** The Country of the Blind
42. **Noam Chomsky** Doctrines and Visions
43. **Jamie Oliver** Something for the Weekend
44. **Virginia Woolf** Street Haunting
45. **Zadie Smith** Martha and Hanwell
46. **John Mortimer** The Scales of Justice
47. **F. Scott Fitzgerald** The Diamond as Big as the Ritz
48. **Roger McGough** The State of Poetry
49. **Ian Kershaw** Death in the Bunker
50. **Gabriel García Márquez** Seventeen Poisoned Englishmen
51. **Steven Runciman** The Assault on Jerusalem
52. **Sue Townsend** The Queen in Hell Close
53. **Primo Levi** Iron Potassium Nickel
54. **Alistair Cooke** Letters from Four Seasons
55. **William Boyd** Protobiography
56. **Robert Graves** Caligula
57. **Melissa Bank** The Worst Thing a Suburban Girl Could Imagine
58. **Truman Capote** My Side of the Matter
59. **David Lodge** Scenes of Academic Life
60. **Anton Chekhov** The Kiss
61. **Claire Tomalin** Young Bysshe
62. **David Cannadine** The Aristocratic Adventurer
63. **P. G. Wodehouse** Jeeves and the Impending Doom
64. **Franz Kafka** The Great Wall of China
65. **Dave Eggers** Short Short Stories
66. **Evelyn Waugh** The Coronation of Haile Selassie
67. **Pat Barker** War Talk
68. **Jonathan Coe** 9th & 13th
69. **John Steinbeck** Murder
70. **Alain de Botton** On Seeing and Noticing